SAILBOATS

BOATS & SHIPS

Jason Cooper

The Rourke Corporation, Inc.
Vero Beach, Florida 32964

PHOTO CREDITS:
© Craig Lovell/Eagle Visions: pages 8, 10, 13, 18; courtesy Star Clippers: title page, pages 7, 15, 21; © Lynn M. Stone: page 12; courtesy Windjammer Barefoot Cruises: cover, pages 4, 17

CREATIVE SERVICES:
East Coast Studios, Merritt Island, Florida

EDITORIAL SERVICES:
Susan Albury

Library of Congress Cataloging-in-Publication Data

Cooper, Jason, 1942-
    Sail boats / by Jason Cooper.
      p. cm. — (Boats)
    Includes index.
    Summary: Surveys the history, uses, parts, and different kinds of sail boats.
    ISBN 0-86593-559-9
    1. Sailboats—Juvenile literature. 2. Sailing ships—Juvenile literature.
[1. Sailboats. 2. Sailing ships.]
I. Title II. Series: Cooper, Jason, 1942- Boats & ships
VM351.C58 1999
623.8' 203—dc21   99–15113
                                                     CIP

Printed in the USA

TABLE OF CONTENTS

SAILBOATS

Sailboats love a stiff breeze that fills their sails and pushes them crisply over the water.

Sailing ships love a stiff breeze, too. They're bigger **vessels** (VEH sulz), built for ocean sailing.

For nearly 5,000 years, all boats and ships were driven by oars, paddles, or sails. Those vessels were used to carry cargo or passengers, or they were used in warfare.

Sailing vessels today are used for pleasure. Motorboats do the carrying and fighting.

Wind fills the sails of the Legacy *as she turns her bow toward home. The long, needlelike pole pointing from the bow is the bowsprit.*

SAILING

Those who love to sail love the water and the sounds of sailing. They love the rustle of sails in the wind and the gentle slap of water on the **bow** (BOW). They love the energy of a boat as its sail catches the wind.

Sailing requires great skill. Sailboat sailors learn how to "read" the wind and water. They learn how to master a boat that lives by the wind.

Sailing takes sailors to adventure. It also takes them back into time.

Sailing on gentle winds can be a dreamy time for passengers aboard a sailing vessel.

PARTS OF A SAILBOAT

Boating has its own language. Words like jib, tack, heel, starboard, port, and rig are just a few. Some of the boater's special words refer to the boat itself.

Like any boat, a sailboat has a **hull** (HUHL), or floating shell. The hull gives the boat its shape beneath the sails.

While the woman feeds rope to a sail, the man handles the boat wheel. On large sailboats, a wheel, rather than a tiller, works with the boat's rudder to steer.

The **mast** (MAST), or masts, are poles built onto the **deck** (DEK). The deck is the platform that covers the hull of most sailboats.

Each mast holds at least one sail. Each sail is like a giant sheet. It's usually made of a man-made material, such as dacron. Different kinds of sails have names like mainsail and jib.

Sails can be open to catch the wind or rolled up. A sailor controls the position of sails with ropes. Together, the ropes, sails, and poles on a sailboat are its **rigging** (RIG ing).

A sailor may go to great lengths to help balance the sailboat. "Hiking" brings more weight to one side of the boat. Note the life jacket and safety line.

A flock of mute swans pays no attention as a catboat sails quietly nearby in the mouth of the Connecticut River.

*Sailboat races are called regattas. These sailboats are racing on
Lake Wanaka in New Zealand.*

The centerboard, or **keel** (KEEL), is a broad, flat structure under the hull. It sticks down into the water like a stiff shark fin. It helps keep the boat steady in wind.

The rudder is a narrow, boardlike structure. It's also beneath the hull at the **stern** (STURN), or rear of the boat.

The rudder moves back and forth to steer the boat. A sailor controls the rudder by a long handle, the **tiller** (TIL ur), or by a wheel.

14

Poles called booms and gaffs support the tops and bottoms of the sail. Together, a sailboat's masts, gaffs, and booms are called spars.

HOW A SAILBOAT WORKS

Sails are slightly curved, like a very shallow pouch, to catch the wind.

Sailboats can sail with the wind behind them, of course. That's called running. But they can also sail forward with the wind to one side. That's **reaching** (REECH ing), and it's the fastest way to sail.

A sailboat can also sail forward into the wind if it can find the proper angles. This zig-zag course is **tacking** (TAK ing). It requires great skill by the sailor.

Beauty on the sea, the four-masted Polynesia runs with the wind.

EARLY SAILBOATS

The Egyptians invented sails for their boats 5,000 years ago. Sailing became easier about 800 years ago when the rudder was invented.

By 1400, shipbuilders had learned to construct ships with several sails and masts. The *Santa Maria,* which Christopher Columbus sailed to the New World in 1492, was one of the most famous of old sailing ships.

La Violente, *a two-masted French schooner, prowls the blue seas off Fiji in the South Pacific.*

CLIPPER SAILBOATS

Clippers, first built by American shipbuilders, were long and sleek. Above their decks were great clouds of sails, as many as 35.

The *Great Republic* was the largest of the clippers at 335 feet (100 meters). The fastest clippers traveled at more than 20 miles per hour (32 kilometers per hour), faster than some modern cargo ships.

The largest sailing ship ever built was a five-masted German ship in 1902. But by then, sailing ships were rapidly giving way to steamships. Steamships were bigger, faster, and safer.

This modern-day clipper borrowed her grand design from the 19th-century clipper ships. They earned the name because they clipped away the miles faster than other ships.

KINDS OF SAILBOATS

Sailboats come in many sizes. They are usually placed in a group by their size and the way their sails are rigged.

Some of the best-known sailboats are the one-masted catboats and sloops. They are used mainly on lakes, rivers, and bays where the water is calm.

The two-masted yawls, ketches, and schooners are larger boats. They can sail on the ocean.

Tall-masted ships, like the famous clippers of old, are big, ocean going vessels. Some look very much like the old clippers.

GLOSSARY

bow (BOW) — the front portion of a boat or ship

deck (DEK) — the covered area across the top of a ship or boat hull; any one of the platforms, or floors, built above the bottom of a hull

hull (HUHL) — the floating shell of a boat or ship

keel (KEEL) — the fin-like structure under a boat or ship that helps steady it against wind; the center board

mast (MAST) — a pole that holds one or more sails on a sailboat

reaching (REECH ing) — sailing with the wind blowing toward the side of a sailboat

rigging (RIG ing) — the mast, ropes, and poles of a sailboat

stern (STURN) — the rear portion of a boat or ship

tacking (TAK ing) — sailing more or less into the wind on a zig-zag course

tiller (TIL ur) — the handle that a sailor uses to control the rudder of a boat

vessel (VEH sul) — a boat or ship

INDEX

FURTHER READING

Find out more about sailboats with these helpful books:

- Brodie, Ian and Goodman, Di. *Learning to Sail.* International Marine, 1994
- Butterfield, Moira. *Look Inside Cross Sections Ships.* Dorling Kindersley, 1994
- Graham, Ian. *Boats, Ships, Submarines and Other Floating Machines.* Kingfisher, 1993
- Humble, Richard. *Submarines and Ships.* Viking, 1997